THE
CONFIDENCE
COACH

A Pocket Coach

THE CONFIDENCE COACH

DR SARAH JANE ARNOLD

Michael O'Mara Books Limited

First published in Great Britain in 2018 by
Michael O'Mara Books Limited
9 Lion Yard
Tremadoc Road
London SW4 7NQ

A CIP catalogue record for this book is available from the British Library.

Papers used by Michael O'Mara Books Limited are natural, recyclable products made from wood grown in sustainable forests. The manufacturing processes conform to the environmental regulations of the country of origin.

ISBN: 978-1-78243-916-5 in hardback print format
ISBN: 978-1-78929-014-1 in ebook format

1 2 3 4 5 6 7 8 9 10

www.mombooks.com
Follow us on Twitter @OMaraBooks

Cover design by Ana Bjezancevic
typeset by Amy Lightfoot

Printed and bound in China

This book is dedicated to my partner, Mine – an inspiring human being; a kind and courageous soul

CONTENTS

'Wheresoever you go,
go with all your heart.'

CONFUCIUS

INTRODUCTION

What is confidence? There's a lot of misleading information out there – many myths, beliefs and expectations – about what confidence is and how we're supposed to build it. It can leave us feeling stuck, inadequate, stressed and confused! To clarify this important issue, I will highlight first what confidence is *not*. Then I will offer a clear, concise definition of what confidence *is* – from a psychologically informed perspective.

Confidence is not narcissism. It doesn't involve extreme self-interest or egotistical self-admiration. It's very different from 'apparent competence' – i.e., when someone *seems* capable and able to cope on the outside, but they're struggling and feeling distressed on the inside.

Genuine confidence does not involve pretence. It cannot be built through the 'fake-it-til-you-make-it' approach, which suggests that by pretending to do things with confidence, you can develop confidence. This approach contributes to inauthenticity (not being yourself), shame and self-judgement, because it infers that it's *not okay* to feel unconfident, it's *not okay* not to know, or to find some things difficult, and it's *not okay* to make mistakes – when in fact the opposite is true.

Genuine confidence, by contrast, is unpretentious and authentic. It involves three key aspects, and it takes time to develop. When *all* of the following aspects are present, we can say that a person possesses genuine confidence:

- **A feeling** of self-assurance, with a sense of trust in yourself, courage and competence.

- **An attitude** that we can have faith in – and rely on – ourselves. There is an appreciation of our own abilities and qualities, and a belief (or hope) that we can achieve a goal, perform well and succeed. There is a willingness to try, an openness to experience and constructive self-talk (thoughts about yourself, others and situations).

- **An action** – actually doing something unfamiliar and challenging. Typically, there's the chance of success or failure, and the outcome may be uncertain.

Confidence is often context-dependent. We can be confident in some areas, and not in others – and with certain people more than others. We might feel confident at work, but far less confident socially, for example. Confidence can fluctuate in accordance with other changeable factors, too, such as stressful external events and our internal experiences (i.e., emotions, thoughts and how the body feels physically).

◆ DEVELOPING CONFIDENCE ◆

We're not born confident. Confidence is a skill that develops through *social learning* – our experiences and relationships with others (family members, teachers, friends, partners, strangers, colleagues, etc.)

We learn a lot about confidence via *modelling* (observing others). In childhood, we watch how our care-givers (and others around us) conduct themselves in response to life's challenges – for example, their ability to manage stress and anxiety or their willingness to try new things. We develop ideas about what's safe and what isn't, who we are, what the world is like, what others are like, what we can do and what we can't do.

Our interactions with others shape our emerging sense of self and confidence. If we're not supported in trying new things – or we're not taught how to cope with the consequences (the outcomes, thoughts, strong feelings and sensations) of trying – then naturally we'll prefer to 'stay safe' in our comfort zone. If we try new things, and our experience is perceived as positive, then we'll want to do it again and perhaps try more new things. This is a learning process called *positive reinforcement*.

If, as a consequence of trying, we experience emotional and practical challenges that we don't feel equipped to cope with, then it's likely that we'll be put off by the prospect and our ability to build genuine confidence will be limited.

Our personality traits

Our existing personality does, of course, influence the development of our confidence because it impacts upon our perception of things and how we behave. Personality traits all play their part. For instance, if someone is very shy, they dislike change, they're not open to new experiences and they worry a lot, then it's likely that these personality traits will negatively impact upon their ability to build confidence – *if* no new social learning occurs. However, our personality need not predetermine our ability to build genuine confidence! This is because how we respond to our emotions, how we perceive events, ourselves, others and the world, and how we behave, **can change**. With practical guidance, emotional support, time and practice, we can learn a variety of new skills that can positively influence our personality and make it easier for us to build genuine confidence.

All of us can develop genuine confidence – even if our personality means that we might find this difficult at first. It can be developed in our younger years, or later on in life – whether we're an **extrovert**, an **introvert** or an **ambivert**. Simply put: extroverts tend to be outgoing, seek external stimulation, and draw their energy from others; introverts tend to focus more on their internal world, and draw their energy from time alone; ambiverts have an equal balance of extroversion and introversion. It's a common misconception that extroverts are confident and that introverts are not confident – all people can develop the skills needed to build genuine confidence. You can become an extrovert with genuine confidence, an introvert with genuine confidence, or an ambivert with genuine confidence!

The process of building genuine confidence takes time. We're aiming to get to a point where we can experience the feeling of being confident, the attitude of being confident and the action associated with being confident in a particular context. To begin with, we need two key things:

- The *willingness to try* something unfamiliar.

- The action of confidence. That is, *actually doing something* unfamiliar and challenging.

The formula for building confidence then becomes quite standard:

1. Choose to put yourself in the position where you can learn (be taught) the skill or skills that you seek, either through face-to-face instruction with a teacher, or learning through observation, self-directed study, such as reading or watching tutorials, etc. Try to have a clear sense of *why* you're doing what you're doing – know your intention.

2. Try, keep trying, learn more, make mistakes, practise and apply your new skills.

3. Reflect upon what happens when you try (the outcomes) and alter your way of being accordingly.

4. Practise some more (as much or as little as needed), until you can apply your new skills effectively.

Throughout this process, it's important to remind yourself that it's okay to lack some skills, knowledge and experience right now. You *can* learn with time, good teaching, patience, compassion and encouragement. Don't expect yourself to feel self-assured initially. In fact, it can be helpful to expect the opposite! You may well feel anxious and really unconfident initially – and that's okay! It's completely normal. If you've had little or no experience of doing a particular thing, then the chances are you won't *feel* confident doing it! What's essential is being willing to try. It's essential for building confidence.

▲ ▲ ▲

◆ NOTICING WHAT IS NEEDED ◆

Genuine confidence is a sought-after, adaptive experience that's linked with our desires and values. It can help us to pursue our ambitions, perform better, achieve our goals and experience a greater sense of fulfillment and well-being in various areas of our lives. It can positively impact our:

- interpersonal relationships (friendships, social life, parenting and romantic relationships)

- work/career

- education

- leisure time

- physical and psychological health

- personal development

- spirituality (if applicable)

- role in community life.

▲▲▲

With this in mind, now consider **what you would like to build your confidence for.** (We always want it for something).

Imagine that you go to sleep tonight and a miracle happens. You don't know it, but you have been given 'the gift of confidence'. When you wake up, you don't know that this has happened. What might be different, in how you think, feel or act, that might cause you to realize that you're now more confident?

Keep a personal notebook close to hand whilst you engage with this book, so that you can consider your answers to these prompts and questions, and others throughout this book. Reflective writing can really help to deepen our self-insight, clarify what really matters, and build motivation for positive change.

Of course, positive change isn't easy. Even if we know what we need to do in order to gain a greater sense of confidence (such as practise something over and over again), the prospect of taking those first steps into the unknown can feel daunting. It can feel like we need confidence in order to build confidence!

The Confidence Coach is here to help you with this quandary. Specifically, it's been developed to enable you to do two main things:

- **Identify and understand, in detail, what gets in the way of you building and enjoying genuine confidence.** It will support you to think in-depth about the stress-related physical sensations, challenging emotions, automatic thoughts, beliefs and behaviours, resistance, and lack of skills, knowledge

and experience that contribute to your
unwillingness to try.

- **Learn more about what you can do to
  address these blocks, and overcome them
  in time.** It will introduce you to some really
  helpful self-help tools, like Mindfulness,
  which will support you to cope well with
  difficult experiences, enhance your self-
  belief, and increase your willingness to try
  new things.

The information and techniques within this book
are inspired by – and grounded in – Acceptance
and Commitment Therapy (ACT), Mindfulness,
Dialectical Behaviour Therapy (DBT) and
Cognitive Behavioural Therapy (CBT), which are
proven to enhance psychological well-being and
facilitate the development of genuine confidence.
You will find some excellent additional resources
on page 121.

With curiosity, openness and the willingness to read on, you can move closer towards having a deeper understanding of your struggle with confidence. With time, patience, new learning, self-compassion and practice, you can become the person that you want to be – the person that you truly are.

With warm wishes,

Dr Sarah J. Arnold

▲▲▲

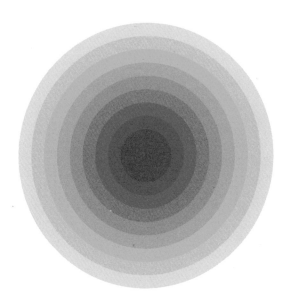

UNDERSTANDING
our
UNWILLINGNESS

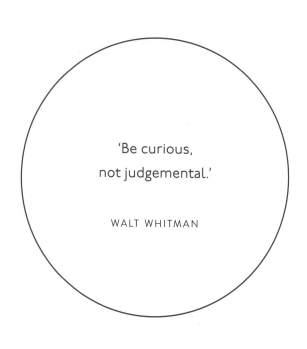

'Be curious,
not judgemental.'

WALT WHITMAN

UNDERSTANDING

our

UNWILLINGNESS

◀ What gets in the way of you building and enjoying genuine confidence? ▶

◀ *What stops you from trying?* ▶

We want to feel more confident, and develop confidence in our abilities, so why do we often hesitate, and avoid doing the things that we want or need to do? It's not always due to a lack of desire. People commonly report that they really want to do X, Y or Z – but they 'just don't'. It doesn't make sense, *does it*? We really *want to* experience or achieve something, but we don't do it.

This occurrence, one that so many of us know, can be helpfully defined as our *unwillingness to try*. From a psychological perspective, this natural inclination – to hesitate and avoid emotionally challenging, uncertain situations that could have 'unwanted' consequences – actually makes a lot of sense.

Simply put, these situations threaten us; they tend to evoke a stress reaction (a host of sensations, emotions, thoughts, beliefs, urges and behavioural reactions) that can feel really raw and difficult to manage. They also highlight the areas in which we lack skills, knowledge and experience (which we don't tend to like much either).

◆ IN THE BODY ◆

When we face the prospect of trying something unfamiliar and challenging, we tend to feel it physically. If we perceive a sense of threat, then it will activate our automatic **flight/fight/freeze** stress reaction, where the body channels all of its resources into fighting against the threat, trying to avoid it, or freezing in it – for self-protection. This stress reaction is hardwired into us, and it's designed to keep us safe. It affects our bodily systems in different and substantial ways.

The **sympathetic nervous system** (part of the body's **autonomic nervous system**) generates our automatic stress reaction and helps to regulate the body's unconscious, automatic functions. This system communicates with our **endocrine system** (glands that produce hormones), which triggers the release of stress hormones called **adrenaline** and **cortisol** that temporarily increase the heart rate, blood pressure and blood-sugar levels, and alter the digestion process – helping to fuel our bodies so that we are ready to fight, take flight or freeze.

If, however, the sympathetic system is activated for a prolonged period of time (through chronic stress for example), it will leave us feeling really depleted. This kind of stress causes the body to respond in the following ways:

- Our muscles tense up – guarding us against pain and injury, and preparing us for action. If this tension lasts for some time, it can result in chronic aches and pains, tension headaches, and so forth.

- Our breathing rate increases (we breathe harder and faster), providing oxygen-rich blood to the body – readying it for action. However, if we take in too much Oxygen, it can upset the natural balance of Oxygen and Carbon Dioxide (CO_2) in the body's **respiratory system** (airway, lungs and muscles). This can cause panic, hyperventilation, pain or a sense of pressure on the chest, feelings of unreality, dizziness and feeling faint.

- Our **cardiovascular system** (heart, blood vessels and blood) enables our heart rate to increase in times of stress. This allows our bodies to receive the nutrients, oxygen and hormones that we need in order to protect ourselves.

- Our **gastrointestinal system** influences how we digest food, absorb nutrients, and how food moves through the body. Stress can affect our stomach (a feeling of 'butterflies', nausea and/or pain) and bowels (diarrhoea and/or constipation). Irritable Bowel Syndrome (IBS) is a common stress-related experience.

It's completely normal for our bodies to react in this way, but it can be an exhausting experience – mentally and physically. If the body is feeling really tired and lacking energy due to confidence-related stress, it can block us from wanting to try unfamiliar things. If we've experienced trauma in the past that's negatively affected our confidence, this can be felt and 'stored' in the body, too – as anxiety, chronic physical tension, aches and pains.

Do you experience difficult
◀ **bodily sensations when you're** ▶
feeling unconfident?

◆ EXPERIENCING ◆
CHALLENGING EMOTIONS

In times when we intuitively feel the need for self-belief – and feelings of confidence – we tend to experience an array of challenging emotions. Anxiety, stress, shame, frustration, sadness, anger, insecurity, vulnerability and confusion are natural and very common.

This happens when we take a risk, step outside of our comfort zone, and face something challenging. Different emotions link with our stress reaction in different ways. For example, anger tends to be associated with our *fight* reaction; anxiety often comes with our *flight* reaction; and feeling overwhelmed, helpless and vulnerable tends to occur with our *freeze* reaction. Once triggered, our emotions have a significant impact upon our thoughts, body and behaviour. However, it's our relationship with them, our perception of them, and our relationship with ourselves when we're experiencing them, that determines what this impact will be.

Many of us don't know how to deal with our emotions well, because we haven't been taught. That's not our fault. Unfortunately, the more we judge our emotions, struggle with them and try to avoid them, the worse we will feel, and the more it will impact upon our confidence.

◀ **Does your relationship with your emotions affect your ability to build confidence? If so, how?** ▶

FUSING WITH AUTOMATIC THOUGHTS

When we face the prospect of doing something unfamiliar that's challenging, the mind will (naturally) think thoughts about it. These thoughts come into our minds as words, sentences, ideas, images and memories – without our conscious control. They will enter, stay and leave the mind, whether we like them or not.

Habitually and automatically, we tend to listen to our thoughts – believe them – and act in accordance with them (a process called **fusion**). Fusing with our thoughts is an essential part of life. It enables us to survive, learn, understand (ourselves, others and the world), develop and sustain relationships, problem-solve, engage with activities of daily living, work towards our goals, orchestrate our lives and live well. However, when our thoughts are influenced by stress, fear or past emotional pain, they can become much less helpful. If we fuse with them, they can stop us from pursuing our dreams, negatively affect our self-esteem, block us from building confidence and stop us from living the life that we want to live. Here are some common, automatic, 'stress-related thinking styles', which can get activated when we want or need to engage in activities that challenge our confidence.

Black-and-white thinking: seeing only one extreme or another, and not the nuances in between. For example, evaluating an experience as a 'disaster', without acknowledging what went well or better. It's a way of thinking that allows us to make quick decisions in times of stress with minimal hesitation. This typically works in our favour when we're faced with life-threatening stress, because we need to react (fight/flight/freeze) quickly. However, with non-life-threatening stress, this thinking style can skew our perception and negatively impact our confidence.

Blaming: often, when we fail – or things don't go as we'd hoped – the mind gets hooked into blaming ourselves or blaming others. We might blame ourselves for things that go wrong, or could go wrong, even though we're not responsible or only partly responsible for the outcome. We personalize the outcome anyway, and think, 'It's all my fault'. We might unfairly blame others too, if we struggle to allow ourselves to make mistakes and find it hard to own them.

Catastrophizing: imagining, fearing and believing that the worst outcome will definitely happen (that we'll fail, be rejected, feel humiliated, etc). This style of thinking is very predictive, and it reflects our fears. In part, the mind is trying to prepare us (emotionally) for the possibility of an unwanted outcome. What's more, it's naturally trying to seek some sense of security, predictability and control in an uncertain situation.

Comparing: comparing ourselves to others. In primitive times, rejection from a social group would most likely mean death. Therefore, doing things *right* and *being good enough* wasn't only adaptive (helpful) – it was essential. Members of the group would look to each other to compare and monitor their behaviour, in order to remain accepted and protected by others. It's believed that this tendency helped early humans to survive. Of course, early humans only had a small tribe of others to compare themselves to. Now, with the internet, the whole world is accessible to us – and we continue comparing ourselves. We're flooded with numerous images of people on social media – presenting the most favourable parts of themselves and their lives. This means that we tend to look at others' best traits and strengths, and compare these with (what we think of as) our worst traits and weaknesses.

Empty positive thinking: attempting to comfort and reassure ourselves with phrases like, 'It'll be fine' – which we don't really believe. This way of coping unintentionally dismisses our experience and blocks our ability to engage in effective problem solving.

Filtering: when we can only focus on the difficult or unwanted aspects of a given situation – forgetting to consider the things that went okay/well and the things that we're grateful for. Our minds are hardwired to focus in on the challenging aspects of our experiences because these are the things that might hurt us physically or psychologically. Here, the brain is actually doing its job – looking past the positives, through to the negatives in order to try and keep us safe.

Mood-dependent retrieval: when we recall memories that match with our current mood or emotions. For example, you're feeling anxious because you've failed at something, and your mind begins recalling all of your past failures too

– along with other things that evoke your anxiety. This associative thinking style is a natural, normal psychological phenomenon. Unfortunately, it can cause us to suffer a great deal – *if* we get 'hooked' by these thoughts and become lost in their story.

Over-generalizing: making inaccurate over-generalized statements about yourself and how things are. For example, something will happen and the mind will say, 'I can't do *anything* right'. In reality – even if you make a lot of mistakes – you can and will do *some things* right. Watch out for this thinking style, it often arises when we're feeling stressed and reflecting upon our experiences. It can really affect our sense of confidence and our willingness to try something again.

Worrying: fusing with anxious thoughts (about a particular task, concern or fear) and replaying them over and over again in the mind – finding it hard to let them go. Sometimes we get stuck – compulsively focusing on the obstacles and difficulties ahead of us – without considering what we can actually *do* to help ourselves and respond to these issues. Worrying serves no useful purpose. In actuality, it worsens anxiety and fuels self-doubt. People who find it difficult to tolerate uncertainty, problem-solve and be assertive may find that they have the tendency to worry.

Self-critical voice: putting ourselves down, criticizing and bullying ourselves. It's a thinking style that often comes up in times of stress, failure and disappointment, and in those times when we're finding it hard to like ourselves. It is the voice of past pain; it's common in those of us who have been abused, bullied, judged, invalidated or criticized by others (parents, teachers, peers, partners, etc.). It's also common in people who've grown up trying to uphold certain high standards in order to feel loved or be viewed as worthwhile.

When mistakes and failures inevitably happen, our self-critical voice gets activated and chastizes us. There's anger in this thinking style, and there may be an unconscious self-belief that this venom towards ourselves is somehow deserved.

Shoulds: regularly thinking or saying: 'I should' – 'they should've' – 'you should' etc. It's a consequence of social learning that creates quite rigid, inflexible ideas, expectations and standards about how things *should* be. It can put unreasonable demands and pressure on us – and others.

▲▲▲

Take some time, at a time that suits you, and reflect upon how your automatic thoughts affect your ability to build confidence. If you're not sure, practise tuning in to them the next time there's a need for confidence and you notice that you're struggling. Approach your experience of thinking with gentle curiosity, and try to get to know what happens in your mind, without judging it or it shutting down. Remember, it's the fact that we fuse with our automatic thoughts and get lost in their stories that impedes us and affects our self-confidence – it's not the thoughts themselves.

These kinds of thoughts are just a normal part of being human, and we can learn to change our relationship with them.

◆ BELIEFS AND BEHAVIOURS ◆

The beliefs and expectations that we hold, about ourselves, others and the world, have a huge impact on our ability to build – and experience – genuine confidence because they directly influence what we do and what we don't do.

Here are some common beliefs and expectations that can inhibit our willingness to try, *if* we fuse with them (which we naturally tend to do).

'I have no motivation'

It's a common complaint – feeling unmotivated. The mind might tell us that we're *too tired*, we *can't be bothered*, or we'll *do it later*. In actuality, there's *always* motivation (intention) of some kind. Either we'll feel willing to try – and be motivated to move towards a chosen goal, or we'll feel *motivated* not to. When we experience that sense of having no motivation, it's usually because our wish *not to* do something is greater than our wish to do it; trying might feel like too big of a risk. Let's acknowledge that poor sleep, diet and a lack of physical energy do, naturally, also affect our willingness.

'I'm not in the mood; I need to feel like it'

Intuitively, we prefer to wait until we *feel* mentally and physically prepared, and we're motivated to move towards our chosen goal, *before* we take action. However, if trying evokes a stress reaction that we don't feel equipped to deal with – then most of us won't feel like taking action! Resistance is a natural form of self-protection. What's more, bear in mind that motivation tends to increase during or after a particular task – as we gain self-belief, develop feelings of confidence through practice, and learn that we can cope with our experiences.

'Anxiety is the enemy'

Many people believe that feeling anxiety is the problem. Common beliefs include things like:

- *Anxiety is a sign of weakness.*

- *I need to get rid of my anxiety.*

- *Anxiety stops me from doing the things that I want to do.*

Whilst these beliefs make intuitive sense, because anxiety can *feel* so threatening, it's not anxiety itself that limits us; it's our *perception* of it, and our *reactions* to it. There are countless messages in our society about anxiety as a 'negative' emotion; many of us were taught that we should 'be strong' (synonymous with suppressing and not expressing our emotions). To cope, a lot of people judge their anxiety, attempt to avoid it, argue with it, suppress it, ignore it, distract themselves from it, and so on. Unfortunately, these control-based strategies tend to make anxiety worse.

'I'm not good enough'

Does this sound familiar to you? Yes? Me, too. As a consequence of our past pain, fears, perception and experiences, this is a belief that many of us have come to share. We look at others in comparison to ourselves, and we experience that deeply felt sense that we're not confident enough, not smart enough, not attractive enough...etc. *If* we fuse with this belief, it can really limit us.

A person faced with the prospect of doing something new and challenging might think: 'I can't do this' (automatic thought). They experience resistance, anxiety and feel tense. They decide not to try, because (unconsciously) they fear and expect humiliation and failure. At their core, they believe that they're 'not good enough' (a belief, and a fear). Trying feels like too much of a risk, because they might fail. If they fail, the mind will view this as confirmation that they're *really* not good enough. This greatly threatens the person's sense of self, so naturally – they prefer to not try (for self-protection).

Unfortunately, not trying tends to create a 'self-fulfilling prophecy'. That is, we protect ourselves from failure, but we also deny ourselves the chance to succeed! These missed opportunities culminate in, and leave us with, an even greater sense that we're not good enough. And, of course, this leaves us even more unwilling to try. It's another vicious cycle.

Many people experience 'Imposter Syndrome' (chronic feelings of self-doubt and inadequacy that arise from trying) when their not-good-enough belief gets activated. It's a heavy burden that contributes to isolation, feelings of shame and so much fear – if it's not spoken about, shared and understood. Perfectionism is one way of trying to cope with feeling not good enough and fearing failure. It involves striving to maintain (unrelentingly) high standards, at all times, in order to feel adequate and acceptable. It's also a way of trying to protect oneself from the psychological pain that would arise if a mistake were to be made. It's part of our *fight* stress reaction.

Of course, it's not possible to live – to try and learn – without finding things difficult and making mistakes. Therefore, perfectionism only causes us to suffer more. Unrecognized perfectionism often leads to social isolation, depression, worry and poor self-worth. It fuels self-doubt, harsh self-judgements and high expectations, and it inclines us to avoid new things – blocking our self-insight and ability to build confidence.

'Mistakes mean that I'm ...'

Take some time, when it suits you, and reflect upon your personal relationship with failure. Here are some prompting questions, which might be helpful:

- Are you allowed to make mistakes?

- How are you with admitting them?

- What does it say or mean about you that you made a mistake?

- What messages did your parents give you about failure when you were growing up?

- How did/do they deal with your failures?

- How about their own failures?

Many of us *will* experience failures and mistakes when we try new things; it's natural and unavoidable; and if we've come to view making mistakes as *bad* and *unacceptable*, and we believe that they mean something fundamentally negative about us, then we will *not want* to step outside of our comfort zone and try new things!

Procrastination is another way of trying to cope (with challenging emotions like anxiety, the possibility of failure and feeling not good enough). It involves avoidance (putting things off), and a sense of resistance (not wanting to) when we're faced with the prospect of doing something. Deep down, we often fear failure or disapproval and feel unconfident about our abilities; we might feel tired and stressed, we may fear what will happen next (fear of uncertainty), or we might simply prefer to focus on more pleasurable things of our own choosing (a wish for control).

Whatever the reasons, procrastination is an example of our *flight* stress reaction, and it can only give us temporary relief from our discomfort. In the long run, it increases our stress and decreases our self-confidence. It can trigger self-criticism, evoke more challenging emotions (like anxiety, guilt, panic and shame), and make it less likely that we'll achieve our goals. Paradoxically, all of this can make us want to procrastinate more because we become really stressed and need a break!

'I need to feel in control (at all times)'

The wish to be – and feel – in control is part of our nature as humans. Unfortunately, some of the habitual strategies that we use, in an attempt to feel in control and find comfort, security and predictability, tend to be unhelpful. For example, avoiding situations that lead to anxiety, procrastination, limiting food intake and trying to do things *perfectly* all of the time.

We get hooked into trying to control the things that we can't control (like the existence of our automatic thoughts), and we lose sight of what we can control (how we respond to our thoughts, feelings and urges – what we do and don't do). To manage the pressure that comes with trying to control everything all of the time (which is not humanly possible), many people engage in behaviours that allow them to, temporarily, completely relinquish control – like binge-drinking alcohol. This kind of coping behaviour typically brings more problems.

'I'm not a confident person'

Many people tell themselves this, as if confidence is something innate that we either have or don't have. Understandably, this can leave us feeling rather hopeless – *if* we believe that our personality is fixed and there's nothing that we can do to develop our confidence (which is simply not the case).

Take some time, before you move on, and reflect upon how your beliefs affect your ability to build and enjoy genuine confidence. Write your reflections in your notebook, and offer yourself some heartfelt praise for acknowledging these experiences within yourself. It takes strength, openness and courage. All qualities that will help you to build genuine confidence!

◆ RESISTANCE ◆

It's a block that we're all familiar with. That strong sense of not wanting to do, feel or think something. It's an important part of our stress reaction that exists beyond our conscious thoughts and emotions.

The mind classifies certain experiences as

uncomfortable, threatening and therefore unwanted, and it encourages us to avoid them at all costs – for our own protection. We can also experience resistance to trying new things that we know would be good for us. It happens for the same reason. Although we don't like to feel stuck, unconfident, anxious, depressed, etc., it can come with a seductive sense of predictability and certainty that feels familiar, and therefore *safe*.

Another trigger for resistance can be fear of success. Success means us getting what we want – and that can feel really scary, because then we will have something that we really don't want to lose. The prospect of our success can intimidate us just as much as the prospect of not succeeding.

Pause now and reflect upon everything that happens for you when you feel stressed and unconfident. To practise confidence as an action, notice how mentally and physically draining it can be. Look at what we often need to manage in order to do this!

There are, of course, *benefits* to our unwillingness:

- We do things that we already know that we can do, and we feel competent and capable when doing these things; it protects and preserves our sense of self.

- Life becomes relatively predictable, and uncertainty is minimized.

- Our beliefs, expectations and core fears aren't activated so frequently, if at all, therefore the raw accompanying emotions aren't felt as much either.

Unfortunately, along with benefits there are *costs* to our unwillingness, too; experiences we lose out on:

- Attaining a sense of competence and mastery (comprehensive knowledge or skill in a particular subject or activity).

- Experiencing pleasure, enjoyment and a sense of personal fulfillment in areas of life that deeply matter to us.

- Developing self-sufficiency and a sense of personal freedom (as our comfort zone begins to expand).

- Building courage and self-efficacy (belief in our ability to accomplish a task and succeed).

- Developing adaptive new beliefs about ourselves.

- Boosting our health and energy.

- Building motivation for more positive change.

- Learning to trust in ourselves (that we can tolerate, and effectively respond to, challenging thoughts, feelings, sensations and situations that arise) when we try, and believing that we can cope (with the potential outcomes). This facilitates emotional stability and effective anxiety management.

- Learning how to trust in the process. Understanding that we will either succeed, or accept the outcome and survive. Situation permitting, we can choose to try again.

- Cultivating realistic expectations (for ourselves and others); giving ourselves and others permission to be human and make mistakes.

- Accepting and understanding our past failures, and learning from them.

- Experiencing a reduction in anxiety (when desensitization occurs).

- Experiencing a reduction in self-doubt (as skills develop and self-belief strengthens).

- Becoming more flexible and adaptable in our thoughts and actions.

- Building assertiveness skills.

- Enhancing awareness of our boundaries, knowing our stance on risk-taking, cultivating good judgement, and gaining clarity about our values, sense of purpose and goals.

As you can see, unwillingness has *many* more *costs* than benefits. **Which of these costs would you like to turn into benefits – as you befriend your resistance and increase your willingness to try?** Note them down; it may help to clarify your goals and personal values.

▲▲▲

◆ KNOWLEDGE, SKILLS ◆ AND EXPERIENCE

Stress-related bodily sensations, emotions, thoughts and behavioural reactions need not block us from building confidence, *if* we know how to respond to them. When we gain the knowledge, skills and experience that we need, we learn that we can cope with feeling unconfident and we can do the things that we want/need to do. There are several core concepts and practical self-help tools that enable us to build confidence, because they help us to cope better with unfamiliar and challenging situations. These are:

- The concept of value-based living.

- Mindfulness.

- Learning how to cope well with mistakes and failures.

- Practical problem-solving skills.

- Assertiveness skills.

- Supportive relationships.

Shortly, I will introduce you to these topics, and give you a sense of how you can help yourself to feel more confident.

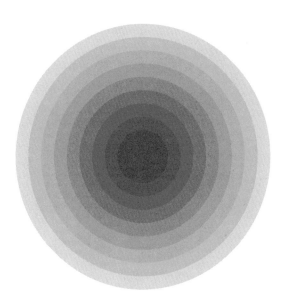

INCREASING

our

WILLINGNESS

'What you seek is seeking you.'

RUMI

INCREASING
our
WILLINGNESS

Now that we've gained insight into some of the key experiences that block us from building and enjoying genuine confidence, we want to turn the focus of our attention to what we *can do* to help ourselves and our situation. If we can make the risks associated with trying feel less frightening – by imbuing ourselves with helpful skills, new knowledge and experiences – then we will feel a little more willing to take steps outside of our comfort zone.

Trying anything even slightly unfamiliar and challenging will still feel daunting, and it will probably evoke stress, but you can support yourself to feel more able – and prepared – to cope well with your experiences. This will help you to build genuine confidence.

◆ THE CONCEPT OF VALUE-BASED LIVING ◆

Many of us know what it's like to move through life on autopilot, aiming for arbitrary goals that we think we *should* achieve. Once we complete the goal of getting that qualification, that job, that house, that car, etc., we move on to the next thing. Goal after goal, these achievements can leave us feeling empty – without any real sense of personal fulfillment – *if* they're not underpinned by our values (ongoing principles that really matter to us). If we're not being authentic and honest with ourselves, it can really hinder our ability to build genuine confidence. This is where focusing on our values is useful.

'Value-based living', also known as value-based action, is a transformative concept that comes from Acceptance and Commitment Therapy. It's a way of being and living that helps us to:

- know who we are

- come to like who we are

- feel motivated to act upon the things that really matter to us

- focus on the things that we can control

- develop genuine confidence.

Authentic, value-based living facilitates genuine self-worth and feelings of fulfillment. It positively impacts how we choose to spend our time, nurtures our self-esteem, encourages personal autonomy, and it develops self-efficacy – all of which help us to become more confident. Here's a useful exercise for value-based living.

Take a look at the following values and select some that matter most to you – at the moment

– within the context of your life now. Then shine the spotlight of your attention on these values for the next seven days:

◆ Friendship ◆

◆ Reliability ◆

◆ Respect ◆

◆ Forgiveness ◆

◆ Fun ◆

◆ Control ◆

◆ Beauty ◆

◆ Friendliness ◆

◆ Authenticity ◆

◆ Bravery ◆

◆ Acceptance ◆

◆ Activity ◆

◆ Freedom ◆

◆ Reciprocity ◆

◆ Adaptability ◆

◆ Patience ◆

◆ Personal growth ◆

◆ Self Respect ◆

◆ Adventure ◆

◆ Assertiveness ◆

◆ Community ◆

◆ Connection ◆

◆ Autonomy ◆

◆ Caring ◆

◆ Charity ◆

◆ Determination ◆

◆ Dependability ◆

◆ Contribution ◆

◆ Discipline ◆

◆ Gratitude ◆

◆ Excitement ◆

◆ Fairness ◆

◆ Challenge ◆

◆ Commitment ◆

◆ Fitness ◆

◆ Cooperation ◆

◆ Creativity ◆

◆ Willpower ◆

◆ Wisdom ◆

◆ Self-compassion ◆

◆ Compassion ◆

◆ Curiosity ◆

◆ Generosity ◆

◆ Hard work ◆

◆ Empathy ◆

◆ Encouragement ◆

◆ Honesty ◆

◆ Self-care ◆

◆ Loyalty ◆

◆ Self-respect ◆

◆ Effectiveness ◆

◆ Equality ◆

◆ Love ◆

◆ Order ◆

◆ Openness ◆

◆ Humility ◆

◆ Humour ◆

◆ Intimacy ◆

◆ Justice ◆

◆ Kindness ◆

◆ Sensuality ◆

◆ Romance ◆

◆ Sexuality ◆

◆ Knowledge ◆

◆ Learning ◆

◆ Skillfulness ◆

◆ Supportiveness ◆

◆ Listening ◆

◆ Meaningful work ◆

◆ Mindfulness ◆

◆ Non-judgement ◆

◆ Open-mindedness ◆

◆ Safety ◆

◆ Security ◆

◆ Pleasure ◆

◆ Proactivity ◆

◆ Quiet time ◆

◆ Responsibility ◆

◆ Spirituality ◆

◆ Stability ◆

◆ Trust ◆

◆ Rest and relaxation ◆

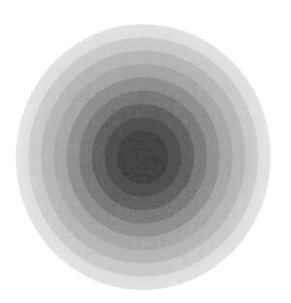

Using the list of values (laid out on the previous pages) as inspiration, write down your chosen values in your notebook. Then set some specific, achievable goals that will enable you to live in line with each value. For example:

Values: self-acceptance and self-compassion.
Goals:

- Try to notice and name my emotions when they arise.

- Practise accepting my internal experiences with compassion, as best I can.

- Try to do simple kind things for myself when I'm feeling emotionally challenged, such as making myself a cup of tea or having a warm bath; perhaps putting on some soothing music and soft lighting; burning aromatherapy oils. Acknowledge my own experience.

Values: **curiosity and openness.**
Goals:

- Watch 'TED Talks' online, and documentaries, in the evenings about topics that interest me (aim for two this week).

- Try a guided mindfulness meditation and notice – with curiosity – what thoughts and feelings come up.

Value: **connection**
Goal:

- Message someone that I care about this week, and check in to see how they are. Let them know that I'm thinking about them.

▲▲▲

Give yourself time to really think about this. You may need to reconnect with your values; you might want to take some time to establish what they are. Remember, your values are the principles that you want to make your life about. These are not things that you think you *should* be; they are qualities that you're genuinely interested in embracing for yourself. There's a commitment to doing this, in spite of the fear that it may evoke, because you can – and because you want to. You're supporting your mind to understand that fear and resistance are *natural* and *normal*, but they need not stop you.

Try to focus your intention on what you *can* do and what you *do* want, rather than focusing on what you don't want and what you can't do. For instance, aim to 'practise self-compassion', rather than to 'stop being self-critical'. Set yourself a conservative number of goals, and ensure that they're realistic.

You might notice some unwillingness when you're ready to begin your seven-day value-based living experience. This is completely normal! It's a new way of being that's unfamiliar. See if you can greet your resistance warmly and thank your mind for trying to protect you from the unknown. Remind yourself that you're choosing to open yourself up to all of your experiences, the pleasant and more difficult ones, so that you can live the life that you want to live. There are skills and ways of being that you can learn (such as mindfulness) that will help you to do this.

◆ INTRODUCING MINDFULNESS ◆

Mindfulness is an ancient practice from Buddhist roots. It's a skill, and a way of being, that helps us to struggle less and cope better with our internal experiences, such as anxiety, resistance, insecurity, uncertainty, and frustration. Mindfulness teaches us how to *receive* these experiences, how to *be with* them, and how to *respond* to them in ways that help us. This reduces our suffering, encourages us to be more accepting of what life brings, and increases our self-belief that we can cope. It allows our values - more than our fears – to guide our behaviours.

Simply put, mindfulness means: *tuning in to the present moment - fully and intentionally - with an attitude of care, compassion, acceptance, non-judgement, openness and curiosity.* Here's a simple introductory exercise for you to try, to begin with:

Take a seat, somewhere comfortable and quiet, and sit upright – as best you can. As you engage with each step in this exercise, try to regard your experiences with a mindful attitude (care, compassion, acceptance, non-judgement, openness and curiosity).

· · · ● ●

Begin by tuning into your body breathing, just as it is. Notice the flow of your breath as you breathe, in

and out. Stay here, with the breath
breathing itself, for a few moments.

● ● ● ● ●

Now, turn your attention to your
mind. Describe your thoughts:
e.g., 'I'm thinking about...'

● ● ● ● ●

Become aware of your mind thinking
thoughts. You're simply noticing these
mental events; you're not trying to control
them, or judge them or push them away.

● ● ● ● ●

Continue to breathe gently.

● ● ● ● ●

Now, turn your attention to how
your body feels; take note of it. For
example, maybe you notice a little
tension in your neck and shoulders?

● ● ● ● ●

Become aware of your emotions in this moment. Do your best to name them, e.g., curiosity, confusion, anxiety and hopefulness. Notice if the mind thinks thoughts about them. See if you can allow them to be here with you, just as they are - just for this moment.

● ● ● ● ●

Return to the breath, and focus on yourself breathing gently once more. Tune into the sensations of breathing. Finish this exercise when you feel ready to.

With mindfulness, we're practising being conscious of what's arising in our internal world – and we're making room for things to be, just as they are. We're not causing (more) suffering to arise by judging our internal experiences, judging ourselves for experiencing them, fighting against them or trying to run away from them. If any of these, very natural, stress reactions do occur, we greet them with curiosity and understanding. We see them for what they are: a normal reaction to fear. We learn to greet our external experiences in much the same way by being fully 'awake' and non-judgemental, moment by moment.

The automatic experience of breathing (gently) is typically used as an anchor to help us stay with our experiences and focus our attention in the present moment. This practice might seem simple, but don't be fooled. The human mind can be a little bit like a wayward toddler – running from place to place, chattering about this and that.

Mindfulness is a capacity that we all have, but it's also a skill that takes time, practice and patience to develop. You can train your mind to become more mindful, and cultivate your ability to focus your attention with daily mindfulness meditation practice. See (p.121) for some additional recommended resources. Keep in mind that you can also practise mindfulness informally – by engaging in any activity 'mindfully', such as eating a meal or taking a shower.

Simply adopt a mindful attitude, and really tune in to what you can see, hear, touch, taste and smell – moment by moment. Mindfully notice your internal world too, whilst you do this. This is informal mindfulness.

Being aware that you feel unconfident sometimes is, in itself, a form of mindful awareness if you can acknowledge your experience with compassion.

There's a great deal of psychological research now that supports the effectiveness of mindfulness. When it's practised for eight weeks or more, it can significantly reduce anxiety and stress, help alleviate depression – prevent relapse, and enhance our general sense of well-being. Along with bringing a greater sense of emotional balance it can enable us to achieve a greater sense of confidence in our ability to cope with life.

✦ RESPONDING TO REACTIONS ✦

Mindfulness is all about learning how to respond to our reactions whenever we're feeling emotionally challenged. These reactions might come in the form of physical sensations, emotions, thoughts, urges and/or stress-related behaviours, as we've already discussed.

See if you can mindfully notice the different aspects of your internal world, the next time your confidence feels challenged.

Mindfulness of the body

It is a useful practice to get into: seeing if you can hold a mindful attitude towards any bodily sensations that you experience. These sensations might include a racing heart rate, sweating, palpitations or tension.

Now when you're feeling unconfident, use your mindfulness practice to notice where in your body you are feeling these sensations and describe them with a sentence in your head. Here's an example for you:

'I'm noticing a fast, fluttery feeling in my chest'.

· · · · ●

Remind your mind that these sensations are normal, they're not trying to hurt you, and they will pass – it's your stress reaction, trying to keep you safe.

● · · · ·

Use your breath to support your mind and body to calm down if you need to. To do this, breathe in through your nose for the count of five – pause for a second – and breathe out through your mouth for the count of eight. (The aim is to breathe out for longer than you breathe in).

· · · · ●

Repeat this for a minute or so.
It helps to restore our natural
equilibrium by re-balancing the levels
of oxygen and CO_2 in the body.

Mindfulness of emotions

Mindful awareness of our emotions is an essential practice. It supports us to understand our internal world, be *with* our emotions and respond to ourselves in a helpful way. There are several core practices that you can begin doing for yourself, which can help to soothe you when you're feeling unconfident and emotionally triggered.

Naming emotions

Learning how to observe and describe our emotions helps us to acknowledge our own emotional experience and identify our own needs. It can feel a bit tricky if you're not used to doing it, but with time, patience and practice – it gets easier. For instance, you might notice frustrated thoughts and tension in your body and say: 'There's frustration'. You may notice that you're on edge and say to yourself: 'I'm feeling anxious'. Try to define your emotions with one *feeling word* per emotion, such as, anger, sadness, shame, anxiety, etc.

Accepting emotions

Knowing *why* we have emotions can help us to accept and understand their existence. Our emotions, as raw and unpleasant as they can be, serve an important function. They're messengers, designed to tell us important information about our internal and external experiences.

Emotions facilitate self-awareness, motivate us, prepare us to take action, enable us to protect ourselves, communicate crucial things to others, and evoke others to respond to us. They need to be evocative in order to get our attention! Different emotions convey different things about our experiences, thoughts and needs, which is why it's so important to name what we're feeling. For instance, *fear* attempts to protect us from emotional pain, physical pain and danger. It warns us that our life, health or well-being could be under threat, and we might lose something or someone that we value.

When we're feeling unconfident and anxious, it's usually because one or more of these fundamental fears has been triggered:

- Fear of death.

- Fear of being hurt physically.

- Fear of being hurt emotionally (such as being humiliated, disapproved of), which threatens our sense of self as worthy, lovable and capable.

- Fear of separation/rejection/abandonment.

- Fear of losing our autonomy/being entrapped and controlled.

Fear prompts us to try and protect ourselves: fighting against the threat, running from it, or freezing (for self-protection). Our reactions are all attempts to escape danger.

Acceptance of something doesn't mean *liking* it – you don't need to like the fact that you're feeling fear. When you're practising mindful acceptance, you are simply acknowledging that your emotions exist, they're real and you're choosing not to fight against them or run from them (because this causes us to suffer more). If we can acknowledge what exists, without judgement, it protects us from escalating our stress reaction. If we continue struggling with our emotions, then we tend to feel emotions *about* our emotions, such as sadness and frustration about our anxiety.

Of course, accepting our emotions isn't easy – it goes against our natural instincts to struggle against what feels unpleasant. Remind yourself that acceptance is difficult, and that's okay. You're doing the best that you can. Try to breathe with your emotions, creating space for them to be with each breath. You're learning how to replace struggling with acceptance, and this takes time. It's a new skill to practise for your own well-being.

These moments of raw vulnerability, pain and stress can teach us a great deal about who we are, what our needs are, and what we can do to ease our own suffering – *if* we can 'mindfully be' with our experiences and learn from them.

Validating emotions

Validating our own emotions helps to soothe the mind, create a sense of internal stability and enable clarity. Sometimes our emotions are understandable and they make sense to us; sometimes we're not sure why we're feeling a certain way, but there's always a reason why we feel as we do – even if it's not yet clear to us.

Validation means that you are privately reassuring yourself that what you're feeling is real and important. Remind yourself that you are human and you're allowed to feel your feelings. They all exist for good reason.

The acronym 'NAV' (*Name Accept* and *Validate* feelings), also called the NAV technique, can help you to remember these three skills. Remember to pause first, as soon as you notice your emotional reaction, and take one mindful breath. Then try to practise this technique, in sequence, whenever you notice a strong emotion.

Mindful non-judgement

Try to get out of the habit of judging your emotions as 'negative' or 'positive'. When we think of our emotions as 'bad' or 'negative', our stress reactions are escalated, and our emotions feel stronger and louder.

Try now to think of all emotions as simply telling you different things. If it helps, refer to the more uncomfortable emotions as 'challenging' or 'difficult' instead. This acknowledges your experience, without worsening your stress reaction because difficulties and challenges can be managed well and coped with.

Mindfulness of thoughts

When you're feeling unconfident, and emotionally triggered, see if you can check in and identify what your mind is saying to you, about you, and/ or about the situation that you're facing. Can you spot any stress-related thinking styles in your thoughts? Chances are, you may find some.

When you do, begin by naming them, for instance:

'I'm being a bit black-and-white'.

or

'Ah, there's my self-critical voice'.

This simple, yet powerful, technique helps us to *defuse* from the content of our thoughts; that is, notice we're thinking thoughts – that may or may not be helpful – and become aware of their impact upon us.

After you've done this, and un-hooked yourself from the story that your mind's telling you, it can be a little bit easier to respond to yourself and your situation. You might want to pause and reflect upon your thoughts more consciously in order to illuminate your needs, identify what's difficult and decide what you can do about it. Alternatively, you may wish to re-focus your attention back on what you were doing when you noticed the thoughts, or *shift* your attention on to something else that's value-based – if your current activity isn't. Try to retain a stance of compassion and non-judgement when you notice what your mind is doing or saying. It's just being a mind – thinking its thoughts.

More on managing stress-related thinking

Another way to defuse from your thoughts, when they don't feel very constructive, is to observe and describe the contents of your mind in a little more detail. You might notice your mind thinking lots of thoughts about a particular subject, for example:

'I want to accept this job, but I don't know if I can do it. What if I can't? Or, 'what if I mess it all up and they fire me. I will have uprooted my life for nothing...' In response, you might say something like:

· · · · ●

'My mind is thinking quite a lot of anxious thoughts'; 'I'm experiencing self-doubt'; 'I'm having a thought that I might mess it all up – I'm feeling really scared'.

● · · · ·

Try to add in some compassionate self-talk, too:

· · · · ●

'That's completely understandable – I've not faced a situation like this before'.

● · · · ·

Try to be non-judgemental, and stay with the facts. Acknowledge that it makes sense for your mind to keep thinking about this, because it's important to you. Suppressing thoughts will tend to make them even more intrusive and frequent. Greet them mindfully instead, as best you can. When you're ready, you can take some appropriate action if it's needed (perhaps problem-solving or assertiveness might be helpful). Remember that you can bring alternative 'what if' thoughts to mind too, in such a situation, to bring about a different perspective, such as: 'What if I learn something? What if I enjoy myself?'

Mindfulness can be a great help when you're in an unfamiliar, anxiety-provoking situation – you're feeling unconfident – and difficult thoughts pop into your head. When this happens, and you notice that you're no longer present, you're lost in your own thoughts, try to greet yourself with compassion and understanding. (When the thoughts are painful, it can be really hard). Use the NAV technique to respond to your emotions, and practise defusing from your thoughts. Then mindfully re-focus your attention back out – on to what you can see, hear, touch, taste and smell once more. Repeat this process again and again if you need to.

Mindfully notice your needs

Sometimes our thoughts can block us from doing the things that we want/need to do. For example:

'I'm too tired – I'll do it tomorrow'.

This might prompt you to procrastinate on something meaningful that's important. When you notice these kinds of thoughts, try to establish the intention that's underneath them. For instance: 'I'm too tired - I'll do it tomorrow' might indicate that you're procrastinating because you're feeling emotionally overloaded and hesitant about how to tackle the task. On the other hand, it may be that you are really tired and it would be in your best interests to rest now, practise self-care, and do what you need to do tomorrow instead. When you're faced with these kinds of thoughts (which all of us have), and you're feeling a bit torn, try to check in with yourself and ask: Does this urge fit with my values right now? Will it help me to act on this thought? If it feels helpful to fuse with the thought, then do so. If it doesn't feel helpful – and it doesn't fit with your values – then notice this, reconnect with what matters to you in the present moment (for example, perseverance), and let your values be your guide. You are *choosing* how you want to act now, consciously and mindfully – for your own reasons – because *you can*.

It's a continual practice, mindfully noticing when certain beliefs have been triggered within us. It's not always easy to spot them, because they tend to be a little bit less conscious. However, with some gentle reflection and excavation, we can learn to recognize them.

Earlier in this book, we identified some common beliefs ('I'm not good enough'; 'I'm a failure', etc.) that can negatively impact on our confidence and willingness to try new things if we fuse with them. When you notice these kinds of beliefs, reflected in your thoughts, see if you can 'un-hook' from their content and notice the voice that's speaking.

Often, it's *fear* – sometimes it's *past pain*. For instance, you might privately say to yourself: 'That's the voice of fear ... I'm scared that I'm not good enough.' When you do this, it helps you to acknowledge that your past experiences and current fears are influencing your thinking.

You're mindfully noticing what's going on for you, rather than judging it or battling against it. This can reduce suffering, facilitate healing and promote personal growth.

Psychological research highlights that it's easier for us to build new, more helpful beliefs than it is for us to disprove or dismantle old ones. For instance, a person may have come to believe that they're useless. They *could* spend a lot of time focusing on this, believing it, arguing with it, trying to disprove it, and so on. Unfortunately, even if they gather evidence that supports the idea that they're *not* useless, deep down they might still believe that they are.

Alternatively – this person *could* acknowledge that 'I'm useless' is the voice of past pain and fear. They could take the time that they need to process how they developed this belief, mindfully acknowledge it's presence still, and then focus their energy and attention on gradually doing things that will help them to build a new, more helpful belief, such as 'I am capable of doing some things well'. In time, the old belief will hold much less power.

Value-based living can help you to build new beliefs about yourself that will help you to thrive, such as *I am good enough. I am capable. I will make mistakes, and that's okay!* Remember, when you're trying new/difficult things that will help you to do this – start small. Try things that only evoke a little anxiety first, and then gradually work your way up to doing more and more challenging things. This is called **graded exposure**.

▲▲▲

COPING WITH FAILURE,
◆ MAKING MISTAKES ◆
AND REGRET

Sometimes, as hard as we try, things don't work out as we'd hoped. Shame, guilt, disappointment, anxiety, heartbreak, anger and sadness are normal emotional reactions to failure, making mistakes and regret. They're experiences that we all know and share.

Many of us weren't taught how to cope well with these experiences, so we do the best that we can with the resources that we have. Blaming ourselves, blaming others, and avoiding our own thoughts and feelings (or trying to) are some of the reactive strategies that many of us use.

While these strategies might have helped us, in some respects, they typically cause more suffering to arise. The mind comes to view our mistakes and failures as 'unwanted' regrets; they can threaten our sense of self, and evoke a great deal of pain.

Unfortunately, this sometimes blocks us from learning from them.

Here is an exercise for you to try. Take your journal and write down your core regrets in life (so far). For example:

'I regret not being more assertive
with bullies at school'.

• • • • ●

'I regret not doing the things
that I enjoy more'.

● • • • •

Close your eyes, allow the memories,
thoughts, feelings and sensations
associated with these experiences to
fill you. Really connect with what it
feels like to recall these experiences,
and breathe in your pain ... that sense
of failure, rawness and vulnerability.

• • • ●

Welcome any resistance; it's normal. Remember, your emotions aren't trying to hurt you; they're messengers telling you about your experiences, thoughts and needs.

● ● ● ● ●

Now, breathe out compassion and forgiveness towards yourself.

● ● ● ● ●

Remember, there are always reasons why we behave as we do. Perhaps you knew no better at the time. Maybe you were acting reactively; maybe you were driven by fear, a lack of awareness, or past pain. It's not your fault.

● ● ● ● ●

These mistakes do not define you. You can learn and grow from them, and transform their existence.

● ● ● ● ●

Keep giving yourself permission to be human, and, with an open heart and an open mind, see what can be learned from these experiences. Are there any common themes in your regrets, such as being unassertive, or avoidant? Perhaps there are new skills that you can learn that might help you, such as mindfulness – to help you become more consciously aware of your own needs and the needs of others; assertiveness training – to help you to express yourself more effectively, etc.

Once you can 'own' your way of being, mindfully, and you recognize that a particular way of being no longer serves you, it opens up space to try something different – something new, which prioritizes your well-being and the well-being of others. Here are some key things to keep in mind when mistakes happen:

- **Allow yourself to feel.** Express your feelings and acknowledge your own suffering with compassion and non-judgement.

- **Notice what gets triggered.** Adopt a mindful attitude (curious, open, compassionate and non-judgemental) towards what comes up for you when you fear making a mistake, or when you actually make a mistake. Mindfulness can help you to befriend the physical sensations, feelings, habitual thoughts and beliefs, and stress-related urges to fight/flight/freeze that get triggered.

- **Notice and adjust the expectations that you hold for yourself and others.** You cannot get everything right, all of the time. Mistakes will happen - for all of us. It's an experience that unifies us all.

- **Be really honest with yourself about your role, the role of others and external factors.** Stay with the facts, and defuse from the stress-related stories that you mind may tell you about yourself and your future.

- **Acknowledge your own mistakes, own them and forgive yourself with self-compassion.** This will help you to build genuine confidence. You must give yourself permission to fail, so that you can learn from your experiences.

- **Learn how to be less judgemental** towards yourself and others (through mindfulness practice), live in line with your values (see p66) and stand for what you believe in. This helps us to fear others' judgements about us less.

- **Reframe difficult experiences** as opportunities to practise mindfulness and gain self-insight, which enables personal development. Notice the great qualities that you can develop during challenging times too, like courage, strength, trust, compassion, kindness, forgiveness, solidarity with others, appreciation and self-awareness.

These qualities contribute to confidence.

- **Check-in and see what you can do to help yourself or the situation.**

Remember, people that you compare yourself to will be comparing themselves to others too. It's human nature. All of us are walking around with some version of the 'I'm not good enough' story; you're not alone.

Think of others as a source of inspiration. Admire their talents, aspire to develop the qualities that you admire in them within yourself, but don't forget that you have many wonderful qualities too. Practise noticing and appreciating all the things that you can do well already.

▲ ▲ ▲

◆ PROBLEM SOLVING ◆

When we step outside of our comfort zone and do unfamiliar or challenging things, practical worries, concerns and obstacles will inevitably occur. What's more, anxiety encourages us to be naturally reactive. Knowing how to make considered decisions when problems arise is an important life skill. With practice, it can dramatically reduce our general sense of anxiety, help us to deal with specific worries effectively, increase our tolerance of uncertainty, and build up our self-belief that we can cope – and do things to help ourselves – even in the most difficult of times. It can really boost our confidence.

If we haven't been taught, or lack experience in using, these skills, then we won't feel confident (yet) in our ability to deal with uncertainty and practical problems. It's completely normal.

Here are some guidelines for dealing with problem situations that might be of help.

Notice

1. Mindfully, describe your current situation in your notebook, and stay with the facts.

2. Clearly define the problem, and identify its consequences.

3. Breakdown the problem into smaller chunks and select the specific issue that you want to focus on addressing now.

4. Identify your end goal or aim.

5. Identify external factors (such as financial cost) and/or internal factors (such as emotions) that might make it harder for you to address this problem.

Plan

1. Write down lots of different things that you could do to address this problem, and consider the costs and benefits of each option.

2. Select the approach that you want to try (one that's achievable and feasible).

3. Breakdown your approach into smaller, realistic and acheivable steps so that you have a clear sense of what you need to do and when.

4. Reflect upon the external and/or internal factors that you identified. What can you do to deal with them? Incorporate this into your plan.

Act

1. Begin when you're ready, and transform your plan into action.

2. Offer yourself some genuine praise for facing this issue and trying to address it.

3. Evaluate the outcome. Did your actions address the problem and achieve your goal? Do you need to try something else? Etc.

When you're tackling practical problems, *notice - plan* - and *act* at your own pace. It's important to give yourself the time that you need to address what's difficult. Some problems, of course, are harder to solve and it's important to acknowledge this. For additional support on how to cope well with a difficult dilemma, and what to do in a crisis, please see page 121.

◆ ASSERTIVENESS ◆

Communication is a crucial part of life. It determines how we interact with others, how we relate to ourselves, and how we feel about ourselves. There are three main styles of communication: **passive** communication, **assertive** communication, and **aggressive** communication (including **passive-aggressive** communication). Each affects how we think, feel and behave. Assertiveness can be defined as our ability to express what we think, feel and need in a way that acknowledges and respects our own rights – and the rights of others.

We're all born with this capacity. However, social learning can have a negative impact on our ability to be assertive. We might have learned to communicate in passive, aggressive, or passive-aggressive ways because that's what has worked before – or because that's how our parents or partners have communicated. We may feel reluctant to be assertive because we fear unwanted outcomes (for example, many people are scared that it might damage their relationships). We might not know how to be assertive.

Assertiveness-skills training tends to have a really positive impact on people's confidence and sense of autonomy. It enables us to ask for what we need, express ourselves and be heard, develop a sense of our own self-worth, and protect/defend our sense of self in a mindful way – without disrespecting others. The more we practise being assertive, the more willing we will be to step outside of our comfort zone and the more confident we will feel.

Here are some key points to keep in mind:

- **You are allowed to feel your feelings.**

- **You are allowed to respectfully express your opinions and beliefs, if you want to.**

- **You have the right to be listened to.**

- **Your thoughts and feelings matter, even if others don't agree with them.**

- **You are allowed to change your mind.**

- **You are allowed to say 'I don't understand'.**

- **You are allowed to make mistakes, and you can learn to own them when they happen.**

- **You can choose to say 'yes', and 'no', for yourself.**

- **You can set your own boundaries, according to what feels comfortable for you.**

- **You can choose to behave in a manner that you respect, and that respects the rights of others.**

- **You are allowed to walk away from situations and people that harm your well-being.**

When we're being assertive, we embody these beliefs. We recognize that others have exactly the same rights as us, and our way of being towards them reflects this.

Sometimes we don't know how to respond in a given moment, and that's okay. Give yourself a moment to think. Take a mindful breath, pause and look inwards. Ask yourself these questions:

◀ *What do I really think about this?* ▶

◀ *How do I feel about this?* ▶

◀ *Is there anything I need or want to say in response to this?* ▶

◀ *What do I want or need to do now?* ▶

Try to be as open, honest, empathetic and respectful as possible in your communications, and express your opinions/requests as clearly as possible. Use 'I...' statements such as:

- *'I think ...'*

- *'I feel ...'*

- *'I would like ...'*

Really try to listen to what is said back in reply. Avoid blaming statements, which can evoke defensiveness from the other person and shut down the conversation. Try to stay with the facts, as much as possible. Be mindful of your tone, the volume at which you're speaking and your body language whilst you're speaking. Try to speak at a normal volume, avoid sarcasm and raising your voice, offer good eye contact, and maintain open body language which reflects your willingness to communicate in a constructive, non-threatening way. If you're not expressing yourself respectfully, then you're not being assertive.

▲ ▲▲

SUPPORTIVE
◆ INTERPERSONAL ◆
RELATIONSHIPS

Choose to spend your time with honest, kind, caring and receptive people who will champion you and celebrate your achievements. Secure, supportive interpersonal relationships help us to trust ourselves and others and build confidence; they positively impact upon our willingness to try new things, how we view ourselves (self-esteem) and how we talk to ourselves (self-talk).

Abusive, invalidating and critical relationships can cause us a great deal of emotional pain; they can damage our sense of self, and significantly inhibit our confidence. Seek out and open your mind to different kinds of people, who share your outlook. Friendly coffee shops, online sites (like www.meetup.com), sports, evening classes, etc., provide opportunities to meet others. It's normal to feel anxious about the prospect of meeting new people; for many of us, it's a step outside of our comfort zone, but it can be a wonderful step, when you're willing to take it.

Building genuine confidence takes time, courage, practice and lots of self-compassion, but it's possible! With the concepts and techniques described in this book, you can learn how to do this – step-by-step. Once you understand your unwillingness, validate it, befriend your fears and learn how to cope well with the consequences of trying, then the act of trying becomes much less scary. You never know, it might just become something that you actually want to do!

▲▲▲

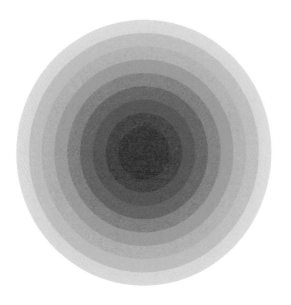

HELPFUL
RESOURCES

HELPFUL RESOURCES

Acceptance and Commitment Therapy (ACT) self-help tools:

Harris, R. *The Confidence Gap: From Fear to Freedom.* Penguin Group, 2010

Harris, R. and Aisbett, B. *The Illustrated Happiness Trap: How to Stop Struggling and Start Living.* Robinson, 2014

www.thehappinesstrap.com/upimages/What_To_Do_In_A_Crisis.pdf

www.actmindfully.com.au/upimages/10_Steps_For_Any_Dilemma.pdf

Assertiveness training:
www.cci.health.wa.gov.au/resources/infopax.
cfm?Info_ID=51

Help with procrastination:
www.cci.health.wa.gov.au/resources/infopax.
cfm?Info_ID=50

www.melrobbins.com/the-5-second-rule/

Books about mindfulness:
Alidina, S. *Mindfulness for Dummies.* John Wiley &
Sons Ltd, 2010.

Arnold, S.J. *The Mindfulness Companion.* Michael
O'Mara, 2016.

Chödrön, P. *Fail, Fail Again, Fail Better: Wise Advice
for Leaning into the Unknown.* Sounds True Inc. 2015

Chödrön, P. *Taking the Leap: Freeing Ourselves from
Old Habits and Fears.* Shambhala Publications Inc,
2010

Kabat-Zinn, J. *Wherever You Go, There You Are:*

Mindfulness Meditation in Everyday Life. Hyperion Books, 1994.

Penman, D. and Williams, M.G. *Mindfulness: A Practical Guide to Finding Peace in a Frantic World.* Hachette Digital, Little Brown Book Group, 2011.

Siegal, D. *Mindsight: Transform Your Brain with the New Science of Kindness.* Oneworld Publications, 2011.

Williams, M., Teasdale, J., Segal, Z. and Kabat-Zinn, J. *The Mindful Way through Depression: Freeing Yourself from Chronic Unhappiness.*
The Guilford Press, 2007.

Guided mindfulness meditations:
www.franticworld.com/free-meditations-from-mindfulness/

Mindfulness resources from world-renowned professionals:
www.themindfulnesssummit.com

www.youtube.com/watch?v=3nwwKbM_vJc

Managing anxiety and panic:
Powell, T.J. *The Mental Health Handbook: A Cognitive Behavioural Approach* (3rd Edition). Routledge, 2009.

If you have gone through trauma (e.g., emotional abuse, physical abuse, bullying, sexual assault, etc.) and you know that it has negatively affected your confidence, you might find it helpful to speak to a supportive mental health professional about your experiences. You can find a therapist here:

www.bps.org.uk/public/find-psychologist

▲▲▲

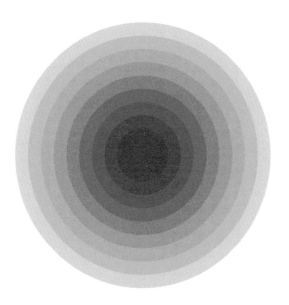

ABOUT THE AUTHOR

Dr Sarah Jane Arnold is a Chartered Counselling Psychologist and author. She works in private practice, offering integrative psychological therapy that is tailored to the individual. She supports her clients to understand their pain, break-free from limiting vicious cycles, and respond adaptively to difficult thoughts and challenging feelings so that they can live a full and meaningful life.

Sarah lives in Brighton (UK) with her partner Mine, their dog Oprah, and Priscilla the bearded dragon.

You can find Sarah at:
www.themindfulpsychologist.co.uk
www.instagram.com/themindfulpsychologist

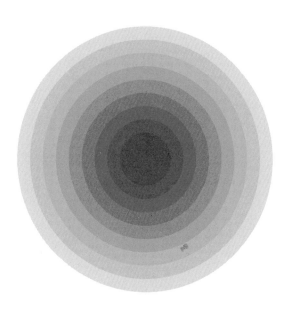